Selia Fox

Copyright © 2021 Selia Fox
All rights reserved.
ISBN:0578978148
ISBN-13:978-0-578-97814-7

AND SO IT BEGINS
MANIFEST JOURNAL

BY

SELIA FOX

The Declaration

What a beautiful and resilient creation you are. Did you know that you can do anything that you set your mind to? Well, it's time that you map this all out! Here is the first step to your journey to abundance in your life.

My name is:_____, and I want abundance in (Check all that apply)

        Self-love
        Forgiveness
        Wealth
        Patience
        Growth
        Healing
        Purpose
        Love

Claim it!

Now seal it with a kiss

Instructions

The instructions are simple, just have fun and focus on you, love. Remember you are beautifully and wonderfully made you deserve all the beautiful things. Protect this book and its contents.

What do you want to accomplish?

Heal yourself

Letters

Is there anyone that you need closure from to heal? It can be anyone mom, dad, teacher, friend, or ex-lover. Dig deep! Well here's your shot. You can send it or not!

Letters

Is there anyone that you need closure from to heal? It can be anyone mom, dad, teacher, friend, or ex-lover. Dig deep! Well here's your shot. You can send it or not!

Letters

Is there anyone that you need closure from to heal? It can be anyone mom, dad, teacher, friend, or ex-lover. Dig deep! Well here's your shot. You can send it or not!

Letters

Is there anyone that you need closure from to heal? It can be anyone mom, dad, teacher, friend, or ex-lover. Dig deep! Well here's your shot. You can send it or not!

This is your time

Cheer Squad

Everyone can use a cheer squad these are the people that love to see you win. Please list them here:

_____

_____

_____

_____

_____

_____

_____

_____

_____

_____

Thank your squad!

All about you

Let's see that beautiful face

You are a picture of beauty inside and out you are creativity, light, and love. Let me see you strut your stuff Pay yourself a compliment.

I am

_____

Zodiac

You are divine just like your sign

Circle your sign

♈ Aries (Ram): March 21–April 19
♉ Taurus (Bull): April 20–May 20
♊ Gemini (Twins): May 21–June 21
♋ Cancer (Crab): June 22–July 22
♌ Leo (Lion): July 23–August 22
♍ Virgo (Virgin): August 23–September 22
♎ Libra (Balance): September 23–October 23
♏ Scorpius (Scorpion): October 24–November 21
♐ Sagittarius (Archer): November 22–December 21
♑ Capricornus (Goat): December 22–January 19
♒ Aquarius (Water Bearer): January 20–February 18
♓ Pisces (Fish): February 19–March 20

Use your strengths

Circle your sign and view your strengths. Write down a couple more strengths.

Taurus Your Patient _____

Aries Your Fearless _____

Gemini Your Open-minded _____

Cancer You have a Big Heart _____

Leo Your Brave _____

Virgo Your a Goal getter _____

Libra Your Fair _____

Scorpio Your Courageous _____

Sagittarius Your Adventurous _____

Capricorn Your Ambitious _____

Aquarius Your a Humanitarian _____

Pisces Your Outspoken _____

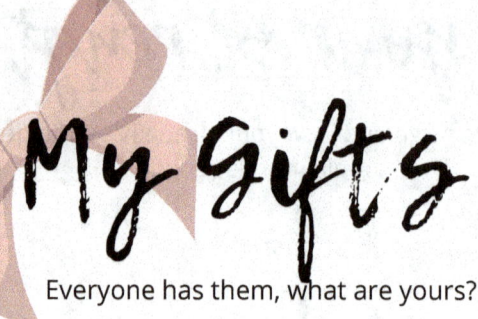

My Gifts

Everyone has them, what are yours?

I am ⟶

I bring ⟶

I open ⟶

I will ⟶

I love ⟶

Change is good

We are constantly evolving, write the things you want to change and how.

What do you want to change?   How will you change it?

Change is good

What do you want to change?   How will you change it?

Write something down you want to change. It can be anything you want my dear ♡

I want to change:
_____
_____
_____

Now rip the page out carry it with you for a week and manifest this

Money Bags

Tips for money

Whether the money your saving is for
a house, car, or just because, saving money is a skill and requires thought and planning.

Tip 1
Pay yourself first - It is a good idea that since you are doing the working you get paid for the work you do. So how much do you plan on paying yourself _____% of my paycheck. Or $ _____ Monthly/Weekly (circle one).

Tip 2
Access the damages- More often we don't even have a plan with our finances. If you don't access the damages we can be paying for products or services we really don't need. So write down all your bills, which one can we remove or lower _____. How much money did that save you $_____.

Tip 3
Create a budget- Stop thinking of a budget as a limitation. Instead think of it as your unique plane that helps you get to your goals. Don't know how, see the budget sheet on the next page.

Tip 4
Stick to it- Being consistent is the biggest factor in being good with money. Don't give up.

Tips 5
Avoid debt- Sometimes we want things while we are trying to save for a goal. Just remember fight your urges to achieve your goals and dreams. You will thank yourself in the end. No afterpay, quad pay, or payday loans!

Money Savers Calendar

Save $5,000 in a year

Week	Deposit	Balance	Done
1	$25	$25	✓
2	$45	$70	
3	$65	$135	
4	$75	$210	
5	$95	$305	
6	$110	$415	
7	$125	$540	
8	$130	$670	
9	$145	$815	
10	$155	$970	
11	$25	$995	
12	$45	$1040	
13	$65	$1105	
14	$75	$1180	
15	$95	$1275	
16	$110	$1385	
17	$125	$1510	
18	$130	$1640	
19	$145	$1785	
20	$155	$1940	
21	$25	$1965	
22	$45	$2010	
23	$65	$2075	
24	$75	$2150	
25	$95	$2245	
26	$110	$2355	

Money in the bank

Week	Deposit	Balance	Done
27	$125	$2480	✓
28	$130	$2610	
29	$145	$2755	
30	$155	$2910	
31	$25	$2935	
32	$45	$2980	
33	$65	$3045	
34	$75	$3120	
35	$95	$3215	
36	$110	$3325	
37	$125	$3450	
38	$130	$3580	
39	$145	$3725	
40	$155	$3880	
41	$25	$3905	
42	$45	$3950	
43	$65	$4015	
44	$75	$4090	
45	$95	$4185	
46	$110	$4295	
47	$125	$4420	
48	$130	$4550	
49	$145	$4695	
50	$155	$4850	
51	$100	$4950	
52	$50	**$5000**	

What do you wish to accomplish in the next 6 months?

What do you wish to accomplish in the next 12 to 48 months?

say it with me

Affirmations

3x's a day keeps the neagative away

This section is for the people that struggle with getting up in the morning with negative self-imagery or negative self-talk. Affirmations can help tremendously with changing your mindset and starting to attract the things that you want in your life. Just like with all things you must believe in the power of your words and the manifestation of your life.

Circle the ones you want to work on. You can write your own too!

- Love
- Life
- Happiness
- Positivity
- Energy
- Stability
- Beauty
- Past
- Strength
- Self-Love
- Future

Life is a journey embrace every minute.

My life is important.

I take responsibility for my actions.

One foot in front of the other will make your path steady.

Life is as big as you make it, and as easy as you think.

See the beauty in everything life gives you.

Make the best of it!

Live life to the fullest.

Every situation has a life lesson, learn from your mistakes.

My life is the best life.

I do what was meant for me, so I have no regrets.

Fear is growth.

I am free.

I choose the life I want.

I oversee my life's direction.

Your turn

List some of your own afffirmations

Love

I am loved and deserve to be loved.

Love is all around me, it nourishes me and uplifts me.

I will give love freely and receive love.

I feel loves warm embrace; I will embrace others with this love.

I will love and respect others.

When I feel the sun on my skin, I will imagine that this is the love of God surrounding me. God's love comforts me.

Love everyone even if they do not want to be loved. They will thank you later.

My heart is open and ready to give and receive love.

I love myself more than I ever thought possible.

I choose what I become.

I surround myself with love and light.

I pour love and abundance into my children.

I love my children equally.

Your turn

List some of your own afffirmations

Happiness

Happiness is everything.

I will not settle for less happiness.

Your friends want to see you happy.

I am happy for my family and friends.

My happiness is the most important thing in the world.

Happiness looks good on me.

My happiness comes from within.???

True happiness comes from within.

My children make me happy.

I am happy with my accomplishments.

I am comfortable with saying no, if it's not for me.

Your turn

List some of your own afffirmations

Positivity

I am a magnet for positivity.

Positivity follows me everywhere I go.

I always look at my life in a positive manner.

Stay Positive.

Give positive vibes.

Baby steps, you got this!

I choose positivity.

I love all people.

I will not judge people.

I am smart.

I am kind.

You can do it!

I am brave.

Your turn

List some of your own afffirmations

Energy

Positive energy flows through me.

I am vibrant and lively.

I put out good energy and get it in return.

My energy is a vibe.

My energy is abundant.

My energy attracts beautiful souls.

Positive energy flows through me daily.

Your turn

List some of your own afffirmations

stability

I am stable and sound.

I attract stability.

I require stability in all aspects of life.

My thoughts are stable and grounded in god.

I have a stable income.

I deserve balanced and consistent people.

My feet are grounded.

I am financially stable.

Your turn

List some of your own afffirmations

Beauty

I am a beautiful soul.

I give and attract beauty.

When I wake up, I see beautiful things.

Beauty surrounds me.

My body is a work of art.

I was made beautifully and wonderfully.

My skin is beautiful, and I love the skin I am in.

My heart is resilient

Your turn

List some of your own afffirmations

Strength

I am strong and can move forward.

I choose to be strong even in moments of weakness.

I am a strong friend.

I have a strong constitution and cannot be swayed.

I get my strength from God.

I have a strong mind and will.

I have everything I need within me.

This will not break me; it will make me stronger.

I am allowed to feel pain.

I am allowed to grieve.

I have a greater purpose.

Your turn

List some of your own afffirmations

Self-Love

I am amazing.

I can see my dreams come true.

I accept my flaws and all.

My light brightens up any room.

I am beautiful inside and out.

I am highly intelligent.

I choose me.

I love myself.

I encourage myself; I encourage others.

I am confident.

I live in harmony.

I believe in myself.

I give myself permission to move on and love.

God is love; therefore, I am loved.

I am consistent.

I love and approve of myself.

I am thankful for what I have.

I am worth it.

Your turn

List some of your own afffirmations

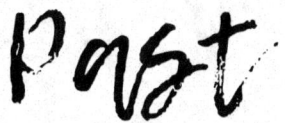

Past

Leave the past in the past.

I learn from my past mistakes.

My past does not define me.

I trust the growth process.

The best has yet to come.

Let that shit go.

Your turn

List some of your own afffirmations

Future

I have faith in the future.

I am open to opportunities.

My future is bright.

Today is a great day.

My future is made of manifestations that I chose.

I look forward to a wonderful life.

My future is so bright.

Just keep living.

I see the future with optimistic eyes.

I set goals daily.

I challenge myself with daily aspirations.

This is my time to shine.

Today is a good day to start over.

I accomplish goals, and it feels good!

Your turn

List some of your own afffirmations

More

List some of your own afffirmations

Affirmation Calendar
Decide what you want to work on weekly

Week 1   Example; Self-love, I love myself

Week 2

Week 3

Week 4

Week 5

Week 6

Week 7

Week 8

Week 9

Week 10

Week 11

Week 12

Week 13

Week 14

Week 15

Week 16

Week 17

Week 18

Week 19

Week 20

Week 21

Week 22

Week 23

Week 24

Week 25

Week 26

Week 27

Week 28

Week 29

Week 30

Week 31

Week 40

Week 41

Week 42

Week 43

Week 44

Week 45

Week 46

Week 47

Word check

Try changing your words and see what happens.

Can't	Can
Hate	Love
Stupid	Smart
Won't	Will
Hopeless	Confident
Bitter	Jovial
Sarcastic	Comical
Conceited	Adoring
Greedy	Earnest
Forceful	Compelling

Words can attract negative energy be careful what you say!

Don't give up

Vision Pages

Here is where you can use tools to create a collage of what you want for your future. Draw use magazines, or anything you can to create your vision.

VISION

Follow the signs

Most of us get signs but we miss them
these signs let you know that your on the right track.

111	Manifest what you want
222	Your on the right path
333	Mind-body and spirit aligning
444	Your angels are guiding you
555	Trust the process
666	Refocus your thoughts on postive things
777	You are on the right path keep going
888	Financial growth
999	Finish your task
000	New beginings coming

NUMBER JOURNAL

Numbers	Details
SAMPLE 111	I was driving and I seen a license plate

graditude

Write 5 things that you're grateful for.

1.
2.
3.
4.
5.

1.
2.
3.
4.
5.

1.
2.
3.
4.
5.

1.
2.
3.
4.
5.

1.
2.
3.
4.
5.

1.
2.
3.
4.
5.

1.
2.
3.
4.
5.

1.
2.
3.
4.
5.

1.
2.
3.
4.
5.

1.
2.
3.
4.
5.

Write 5 things that you're grateful for.

1.	1.
2.	2.
3.	3.
4.	4.
5.	5.

1.	1.
2.	2.
3.	3.
4.	4.
5.	5.

1.	1.
2.	2.
3.	3.
4.	4.
5.	5.

1.	1.
2.	2.
3.	3.
4.	4.
5.	5.

1.	1.
2.	2.
3.	3.
4.	4.
5.	5.

Write 5 things that you're grateful for.

1.
2.
3.
4.
5.

1.
2.
3.
4.
5.

1.
2.
3.
4.
5.

1.
2.
3.
4.
5.

1.
2.
3.
4.
5.

1.
2.
3.
4.
5.

1.
2.
3.
4.
5.

1.
2.
3.
4.
5.

1.
2.
3.
4.
5.

1.
2.
3.
4.
5.

Mediation

Aroma

Lights

Music

Relax

Breathe

Focus

Awareness

Calm

Did you know mediation can help with depression?
Relax, clear your mind, and manifest

Mediation Tips

Create a space
Create a quiet serine place that feels
comfortable spiritually and physically.

Choose a certain time and day
It is best to maintain consistency by meditating
on a certain time and day.

Use Aroma
Candles or essential oils can
bring clarity and curative properties.

Music or Voice Guidance
Remember to meditate in the best frequencey
for you 528 hertz can help with healing.

Breathe
Listen to your breathing slowly and deeply
try counting in your mind breathe in 4 sec exhale
5 sec.

Relax, clear your mind, and manifest

Self-care

Physical - Take care of your physical well-being with something like Yoga, exercising, or even hiking.

Mental- Practicing mindfulness, take a no TV break. Read a positive book.

Emotional- Dealing with stress in a positive manner, practicing empathy, and becoming more aware of your feelings.

Spiritual- Seeking understanding and things that nourish your spiritual self. Meditating and journaling.

Intellectual- Learning more, exploring personal growth.

Did you know that if you place your feet on the earth, it can help align your energy?

Just a few minutes out of the day

Calm your mind

Feel relaxed

I walked ___ minutes on the ground today.
I will walk___ minutes on the ground tomorrow.

Let's see your pretty toes

Are you bored?

Instead of picking up your phone let's calm your mind

Color
Puzzles
Surveys
Read

Your brain is a muscle so work it out!

Book List

Write some titles that you want to read.

Think

Word List
- BEAUTY
- BRAVE
- CARE
- FOCUS
- FUTURE
- GOALS
- GUIDE
- HEART
- LONGEVITY
- LOVE
- MANIFEST
- PRETTY
- QUEEN
- SELF
- SMART
- STABILITY
- STAR

```
                          B W
          E U             S I                 H X
            S T           H M               J V
              P B       P H D N F Q   Z P
                R E F O C U S K G J E
                  E R U T U F L O V E
                Y Y T G U I D E A M B N
                K O T T R A E H V G N
      X C Q H B T Z U Y S T A B I L I T Y E S
      V U S T A R V H A T Y Y T I V E G N O L
                N T U V S E F U J B O H
                  L Q U E E N B S M A R T
                    R F H F W W F L E S
                      I N V I H E V A R B K
            N V       N M C S M G       F N
          A D             A L           F J
        M K               R A             N N
                          E O
                          O G
```

What words make you feel good?

....
....
....

Top 5 favs

Songs
1.
2.
3.
4.
5.

Shows
1.
2.
3.
4.
5.

Movies
1.
2.
3.
4.
5.

Designers
1.
2.
3.
4.
5.

Rappers
1.
2.
3.
4.
5.

Singers
1.
2.
3.
4.
5.

Top 5 favs

Games
1.
2.
3.
4.
5.

Names
1.
2.
3.
4.
5.

Shoes
1.
2.
3.
4.
5.

Things to do
1.
2.
3.
4.
5.

Bags
1.
2.
3.
4.
5.

Holidays
1.
2.
3.
4.
5.

Lyrics

Write the lyrics to your favorite song

Be someones inspiration

Best Frannnn

You:

Name

Birthday

Zodiac

Favorite Color

Favorite Qualities

Best Friend:

Name

Birthday

Zodiac

Favorite Color

Favorite Qualities

Let's see you and your bestie

A friend loves you unconditionally and is there no matter what!
Tell me about your best friend.

_____
_____
_____
_____
_____
_____

Random acts of kindness

Remember you get what you give
Give from your heart and watch the blessing flow.

What can you do to help someone?

1.
2.
3.
4.
5.
6.
7.
8.
9.
10.

Thoughts

A penny for your thoughts

What did you learn about yourself?

MY NOTES

MY NOTES

Your work is not complete use the tools and keep going, never ever give up!

Stay Fearless

www.ingramcontent.com/pod-product-compliance
Lightning Source LLC
Chambersburg PA
CBHW072016290426
44109CB00018B/2259